The Second Listening Book

Loaded Question & Other Stories

James Webb

LIONESS
WRITING LIMITED

For Calvin, Reid, Xanthe, Parker and Imogen,
because there's no way that I'm writing four more of these things...

"We owe it to each other to tell stories."

Neil Gaiman

CONTENTS

ACKNOWLEDGEMENTS

I owe something to each of the following people. Perhaps an acknowledgement in this book will keep them from calling in the debt collectors. In no particular order, I am grateful to and thankful for Derrick Harris, Scott Curtis, Chris & Nerida, Vincent Vincendeau, Dave 'Chiselled Abs' Breen, Max Gove (for countless odd jobs), Rob Wallen and the man who sold me a pear.
Also, thank you once again to Elsa Lewis. Every writer needs an Elsa.

"Take hold of teaching. Do not let go. Watch over her..."

INTRODUCTION

Is it just me or is the pace of life sometimes a little hectic? OK, a lot hectic.

Maybe it's just me who feels this way, that there's a relentless pace involved in modern life, like being strapped to the front of a locomotive. Busy, busy, busy, rushing around, making life work as best I can.

Maybe it is just me. Maybe not.

You know those times, those precious times, where your time is your own, and you sit down with a good story? A book or a film or a television program or music or a video game. We call it 'relaxing' or 'winding down' and we deserve it after such a busy week, right? Well, we more than deserve it. We need it. Because we're not 'relaxing' or 'winding down.' We're feeding our souls. That's what it is. Feeding our souls.

So, what do we feed them? You are what you eat, they say, and they are right. Is it a diet of seductive lies, popular half-truths, meaningless nonsense? Or is it something else? Something with a bit of meat to it, something nourishing?

One day you're going to need some truth. You'll be in the midst of a crisis, either your own or someone else's, and you'll need some heavy-duty truth. If your soul is well fed then maybe, just maybe, from out of nowhere, you'll open your mouth and that punctual truth will come tumbling out. You'll shock yourself, and think, where did that come from? But God and your soul, they'll know.

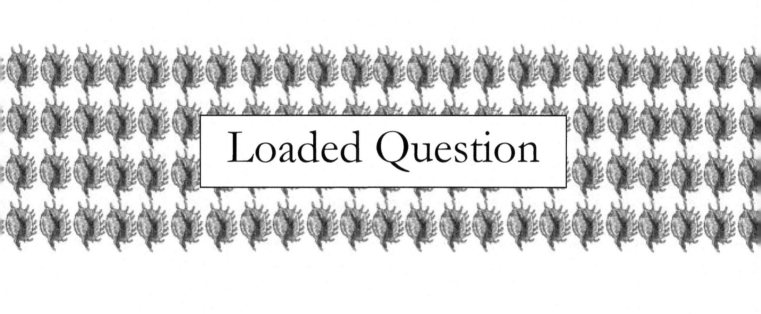

Loaded Question

The man sat down in the middle of the clearing, legs and arms crossed, face like thunder.

The squirrel on a nearby tree watched him, curiosity etched all over its cute little features. When it could take it no longer, it scrambled along the branch, down the trunk and skittered over to the man.

The man watched the squirrel. Actually, glared at the squirrel would be more accurate.

"What are you doing?" the squirrel said.

"I'm waiting," the man said.

"For what?" the squirrel said.

"For a miracle," said the man.

"A miracle?" said the squirrel.

"Yes, a miracle," said the man.

The squirrel thought for a moment. "Why?"

"Because," the man began, "I am sick of God not doing anything. I've waited for Him and trusted Him for a long time, and nothing's ever happened. I've decided that if God exists, then He owes me a miracle, and I'm going to sit here until He does it, and if He doesn't, then there's only one conclusion to draw. Namely, that there's no God."

The squirrel thought for a bit longer.

"What kind of miracle? Something like water being turned into wine?"

"That would do for a start," said the man.

"Well, just over that hill there's a vineyard, and the rain falls, and the vines grow and the grapes are turned into wine. Water into wine. Surely that's a miracle?" said the squirrel.

"Doesn't count," said the man.

"Why not?"

"It's not a proper miracle. It's just something that happens naturally."

The squirrel thought of one or two clever replies, but kept them to himself.

"Well, what about five thousand being fed from five loaves?" he finally said.

"Yes, that would qualify as a miracle," the man agreed.

"Just over that other hill there's a wheat field. All that wheat will feed many thousands of people, yet it all started with sowing some tiny seeds," the squirrel began.

"Oh no you don't," interrupted the man. "I know where you're going with this and it doesn't count either. In fact, it's all I ever hear. Whenever I ask for a miracle, all people ever say is, 'What about this common thing that happens every day?' and I'm fed up with it. It doesn't count. None of that normal, everyday stuff counts. I want a miracle. A proper, bona fide, honest-to-goodness miracle. Something that isn't ordinary. Something that can't be explained by anything other than God."

The squirrel thought of a couple of clever replies to this too, but he also thought about some nuts, and then decided to say something else entirely.

"What about if you saw someone who was dead come back to life?" he said.

"That would be amazing," said the man.

6

"Every day thousands of new people spring into being. They weren't just dead; they didn't even exist! And then, there they are! Surely that's a miracle!"

"You're talking about babies and stuff, aren't you?" said the man.

"Yes," said the squirrel.

The man threw his arms up in the air.

"How many times do I have to say it? IT DOESN'T COUNT. Those aren't miracles, they're just normal things. That's it. I've had it!" the man said.

He uncurled himself, stood up and stomped off out of the clearing.

"I'm done with this. It's clear to me now. There is NO GOD!" he yelled, as he left the clearing.

The squirrel watched him go, shrugged and scampered back up the tree.

In heaven, God rolled His eyes.

"Unbelievable. You mean that a talking squirrel wasn't enough?"

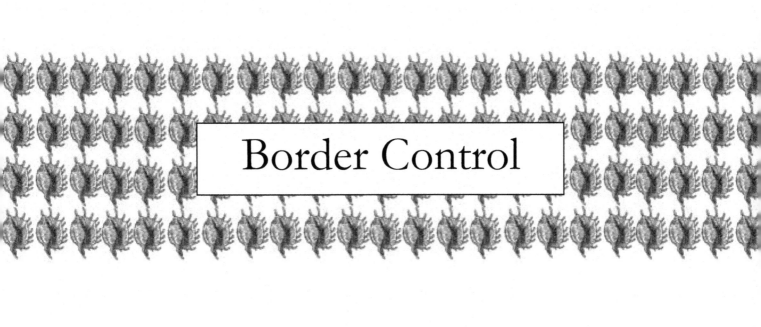

Border Control

The land of Hecbia was a terrible place to live. Its rulers were corrupt, its land was barren and its economy was in pieces. By contrast, neighbouring Blistopia was heaven on earth; a veritable land of milk and honey. The President of Blistopia had a progressive view on immigration and was very happy to offer asylum to those citizens of Hecbia who desired it. Border control was always very busy, with a line of Hecbian citizens stretching back, clutching their Blistopian citizenship documents (signed by the President himself) to their chests.

Each gate was manned by a Blistopian citizen, many of whom had once been refugees from Hecbia themselves. The immigration process was often the same.

"Next please."

"I am here to move to Blistopia," the smiling refugee would say, holding forth his citizenship papers.

"You don't sound like a Blistopian," the border control officer would say.

"I have papers," the refugee would say.

"That may be. You have papers that say you are a Blistopian, but anyone could tell from your accent that you're Hecbian. Please step aside and join the line over there."

The confused refugee would be shuffled off to the side.

"Next please."

"I am here to move to Blistopia. I have my papers."

"I see. Can you sing the Blistopian national anthem for me?" the officer would ask.

"I don't know it yet. I only received my papers this morning."

"But I expect you know all the words to the Hecbian national anthem, don't you?"

"Of course. I have lived there all my life," the confused refugee would admit.

"I see. Please move over there and wait. Next please." And on and on it would go.

"Yes, I can see that you have papers, but you are wearing a Hecbian national team football shirt. Please join the line over there."

"They may have been signed by the President himself, but can you tell me how many children the President has? No? Please join the line over there."

"You have a slip of paper saying that you are a Blistopian, but everything about your behaviour suggests that you are still a Hecbian. Please join the line over there."

The line that most Hecbians reluctantly joined filtered into a detention centre. Above the gate was a large sign that read: "Welcome to Blistopia. Please Behave Yourself." The conditions in the camp were terrible, indeed not much better than in Hecbia itself, but at least it was on Blistopian soil and the refugees still had their papers. If you were to visit the camp you would see it packed with defeated souls, grubby and sad, clutching their citizenship papers, forced smiles on their lips, repeating the mantra, "We're so happy to be citizens of Blistopia. We're so much better off."

When the President visits the border to see what is happening, how terrible it will be for those border control officers.

Signs and Wonders

Langley Farm was enjoying a good run of late. It was just a small place, which produced a small crop of melons each harvest, but it was a good crop. It had started with a few positive posts by celebrity melon blogger Fruity Jason, who had declared that Langley Farm's latest crop produced, (and I quote) '...probably the best melon I have tasted all summer.' Well, things went viral and global and mental for a while, and before long Langley Farm melons were the melons to eat, and to be seen eating.

Success breeds success, so Langley decided that his farm needed a new sign. The old one was OK. It let people know that this was Langley Farm, but it didn't let people know that this was *the* Langley Farm, so a new sign was ordered:

LANGLEY FARM – HOME OF PRIZE-WINNING MELONS.

Year after year, the crop was good. And so it should have been, because Langley was a fine melon farmer and knew exactly what he was doing. He expanded his crop a little each year, but only a little (because quality beats quantity nine times out of ten), and he also made sure to expand his sign each year. By a lot. After all, it pays to advertise, and as the awards and praise built up, so the sign grew in order to be able to advertise each new achievement.

The sign grew bigger.

LANGLEY FARM – HOME OF PRIZE-WINNING MELONS. "CAN'T BE BEAT." - F. JASON, CELEBRITY MELON EXPERT.

Bigger and bigger.

LANGLEY FARM – HOME OF PRIZE-WINNING MELONS. "CAN'T BE BEAT." - F. JASON, CELEBRITY MELON EXPERT. AWARDED THE GOLDEN MELON THREE YEARS IN A ROW.

Bigger and bigger and bigger.

LANGLEY FARM – HOME OF PRIZE-WINNING MELONS. "CAN'T BE BEAT." - F. JASON, CELEBRITY MELON EXPERT. AWARDED THE GOLDEN MELON FOUR YEARS IN A ROW. OFFICAL MELON PROVIDER FOR THE OLYMPIC GAMES.

And on and on and on. There were always more accolades to advertise, and even when there weren't it was always worth making the sign bigger. A bigger and better advert appealed to more people. You could see it from miles away.

Well, as it happens, the sign had grown so big that it, literally, overshadowed the fields. Melons like the sun, and there was no longer any sun, only a huge sign-shaped shadow. So that year there was no crop. No crop meant no melons, just an empty field. And, wouldn't you know it, the awards and praise and accolades soon dried up as well.

Be Careful What
You Wish For

Every Sunday Ruby's parents dragged her to the cathedral service, and every Sunday Ruby sat there on the cold, hard, wooden pew listening to a boring man talk about boring things for what felt like one hundred boring hours. It was the worst event in her week by far, even worse than having to go to school.

She pleaded and begged, but her parents wouldn't listen.

"You're too young to stay at home by yourself," her mother would say.

"Besides, it's good for you," her father would say.

Ruby had been unjustly sentenced to an eternity of boring Sunday mornings, with no prospect of parole.

But one Sunday, out of the blue, things became a lot more interesting.

Normally, after the service, she would mill around the cathedral by herself while her parents had boring conversations with boring people. Sometimes there were other children her age there, but they were usually boring, just like their parents. Waiting to go home after the service was an extra little torture that her parents had devised. To be so close to freedom and yet to be imprisoned still!

On this one particular Sunday, Ruby's wandering took her down a corridor she didn't remember having explored before. The corridor wasn't especially interesting in itself, but it ended in a stout wooden wall, and in that wall was a small, child-sized door. Bored children are dangerous things, and Ruby opened the door.

At first, Ruby was disappointed with what she found. The door opened up into a small, plain boring-looking empty room. There was no adventure to be had here. Why should she have expected anything else? After all, why would there be anything even very slightly exciting in this place where she had to come every week to be bored out of her wits by professional borers?

But the room was not actually empty.

"Hello," said a silky voice from the corner.

Ruby jumped, because she hadn't been expecting this, and she was just about to dash back through the door to the safety of boredom, when something about the voice made her stop.

"Don't go," it said, "I don't often get visitors."

The voice made Ruby think of dripping honey and spoonfuls of sugar and soothing music. Looking around, she noticed a beautiful, sleek cat, licking its paws in the corner of the room.

"Hello?" she said, but she said it quietly, as she didn't want to be the kind of girl who was seen talking to a cat, especially if the cat wasn't going to talk back.

"Yes, hello again," the cat said.

"You can talk," the astonished girl said.

"So can you," the cat said.

"But cats can't talk," said Ruby.

"I think that they can," the cat said.

"No they can't," said Ruby.

"I'm going to have to strongly disagree with you here," said the cat, whose name was Jonas. Ruby didn't know what to say next.

"I say, I get pretty bored here by myself," Jonas continued. "Would you like to play?"

"Play? With you? Of course!" Ruby didn't even hesitate.

This was the most magical thing that had ever happened to Ruby. Playing with a talking cat! It sounded like it should be a lot of fun, and it most certainly was. She and Jonas enjoyed a very exciting game of Hide & Seek, but it seemed as if they had only been playing for a few minutes before Ruby heard her parents calling for her.

Afraid that they would discover her secret room and her secret friend and ruin it all by turning it into something boring, Ruby rushed from the hidden room and bumped into her parents at the end of the corridor.

"Where have you been?" her father said.

"It's time to go home, dear," said her mother.

"Oh, already? I want to stay! Please can we stay?"

"What did you say?" said her astonished father.

"This has never happened before!" her mother managed to utter, just before she fainted with shock.

Ruby's attitude towards the Sunday service was totally transformed from that day forth. Every Sunday she was ready bright and early, before her parents, and she practically ran all the way to the cathedral. Her parents were amazed at this remarkable conversion. But, of course, you and I know the truth. Ruby wasn't keen to get to the cathedral because she was looking forward to the service. She wanted to get there early to squeeze in a game of Hide & Seek with Jonas before the service began. In fact, the service was now even more boring to Ruby, because it stopped her doing the one thing that she really wanted to do while she was at the cathedral, which was to play with Jonas. Sometimes, during the service, Jonas would slink out from a hidey-hole somewhere and wander through the cathedral, winking at Ruby. When he did this, she could barely contain her excitement. Hurry up, boring man talking about boring things, she would say to herself, Jonas is waiting for me!

Ruby enjoyed exciting games of Hide & Seek for many weeks, until one day, after the service, she found Jonas curled up, asleep, in the corner of the hidden room.

"Wake up, Jonas. It's time to play!" she said.

Jonas the cat woke up, blinked at her and yawned.

"Don't want to," he said, before settling down to go back to sleep.

"What do you mean?" said Ruby, unable to hide her disappointment.

"I don't want to play with you anymore. You're boring," said the cat.

Boring? How could he say that?

"You're not very good at Hide & Seek, and I'm bored of you now. Go away and leave me alone," purred Jonas, turning his back on the little girl.

"Oh, Jonas, don't say that! Please, we can try something else! What would make it more exciting? I'll just die if you take away our games of Hide & Seek!"

Jonas regarded Ruby with narrow eyes.

"Well, there is something that might help," he admitted.

"What?"

"It'll make the game less boring, I suppose," the cat continued, to himself.

"Yes, yes. I'll do it! Anything! I don't want to be boring, and I don't want to stop playing Hide & Seek," Ruby said, too eagerly.

"Very well. Here's what you need to do. Next Sunday, come as early as you can, and bring me something to eat," the cat explained.

"Something to eat?"

"Bring me some cheese. I like cheese," said Jonas, licking his lips.

Cheese? Ruby had never heard of a cat that liked cheese before, but if that's what Jonas needed her to do so that she could keep things the way that they were then, well, that was fine by her.

"OK, I'll do it." Ruby said.

"Good. Now go away and leave me to sleep," said the cat, yawning once more.

The next week seemed to last forever, but finally Sunday came, and Ruby sprinted off to the cathedral as fast as she could – even faster than usual.

"Slow down! It won't be open yet!" her parents yelled after her, but Ruby didn't care. She already knew secret ways into the cathedral when it was locked, because Jonas had shown her. Sure enough, waiting for her in the little room was the proud cat. He meowed when he saw her.

"You took your time. Did you bring the food?"

"Yes," said Ruby, pulling a lump of cheese from her coat pocket.

"Excellent. Now you eat it," Jonas said.

"What? I thought that it was for you." Ruby was confused.

"I'm not hungry at the moment. You eat it instead."

A tiny voice at the back of Ruby's mind, a voice that sounded a lot like the voice of the boring man who led the boring services, told her that it would be a bad idea to eat the cheese.

"Come on. Do you want to play or not?" Jonas stretched, arching his back the way that cats do.

Ruby pushed the doubt away. After all, it was a boring voice. She took a bite of the cheese. It tasted good. She took another bite, and then another and that was all it took. The cheese was gone.

"Now, can we play?" she said, through a mouthful of cheddar.

Jonas smiled.

"Oh yes. We can play now," he purred.

"Good," said Ruby, swallowing the cheese. But before it had even travelled all the way down her throat she began to feel a bit strange.

"I feel funny," she said, and then clapped her hand over her mouth in surprise. Was that her voice? It sounded different. High pitched and squeaky. At the same time, she was beginning to feel dizzy. The room seemed to be spinning and getting bigger and bigger around her, and at the same time, her clothes began to feel like they didn't quite fit any more. They felt like they were getting bigger too.

"What's happening?" she asked, in her squeaky, terrified voice.

"You're becoming less boring," said Jonas.

Ruby wiggled her nose. Were those whiskers? Did she have whiskers? Thick fur began to form all over her tiny body, and she knew, with horrible certainty that she was growing a long, thin tail. The sinister truth crept over her, as Ruby the little girl became Ruby the little mouse.

"I only wanted to play Hide & Seek," she squeaked to the cat, as the metamorphosis finally ended.

"Oh, yes, we can play Hide & Seek," sneered the cat. "It'll be far less boring for me now. You hide and I'll seek."

As Ruby skittered off into the darkness, in the grip of terror, she heard Jonas call out from behind her.

"Ready or not, here I come!"

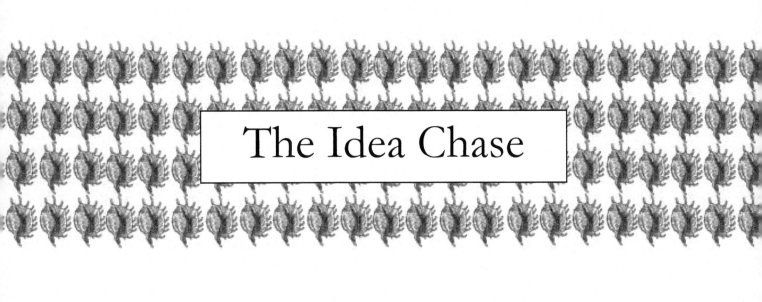

The Idea Chase

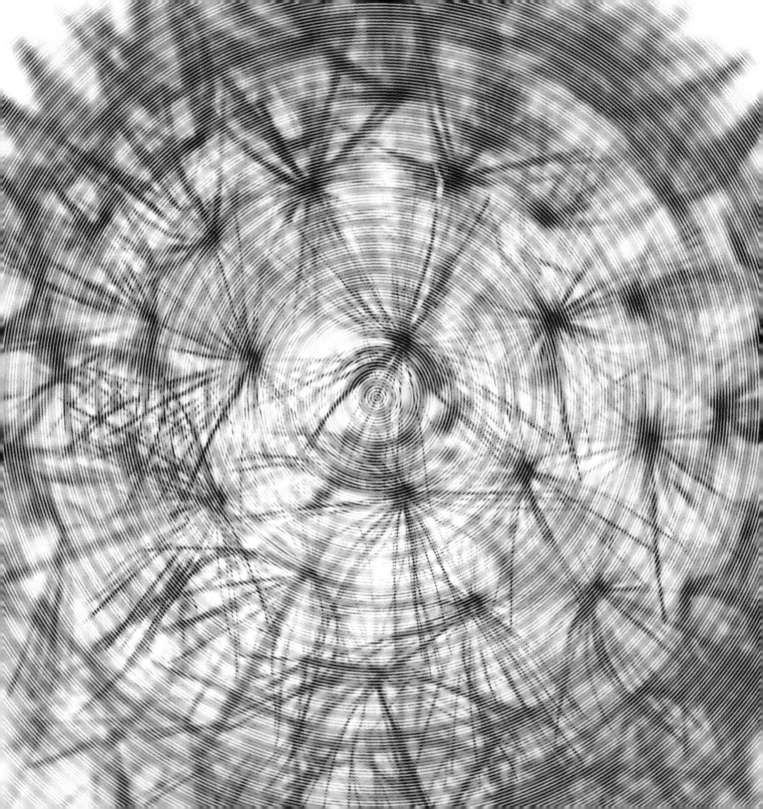

The man happened to look out of his window at just the right time to see it floating through his garden. Could it be? Surely not? The man rushed to his door and opened it to check whether or not his eyes were deceiving him. It was true! It was! An Idea floating right through his garden. He had never seen one in the wild before, and this was a big one!

The man didn't hesitate. He rushed to his spare room, grabbed his Idea Net and fairly sprinted through the house, crashing through the front door and stumbling into the garden. Where had it gone? There! He saw the Idea floating away, leaving his garden and heading towards the forest on the horizon. The man wasn't going to miss this opportunity, so wielding his Idea Net like a questing knight wields a lance, he tore through the gate after the Idea.

The Idea drifted into the forest, with the man hot on its heels. The man's frenzied pursuit took him past an old farmer, who was pulling a small cart full of loaves of bread.

"Can you help me, lad?" said Old Farmer Munchley. "There's a fallen tree on the path up ahead, and I can't get my cart past it. The two of us could have it aside in a jiffy."

"Sorry," said the man, "can't stop. Busy."

The Idea floated out of the forest and down alongside the river. The man followed, waving his Idea Net and panting as exhaustion began to creep up on him. The man was so focused on following the swiftly-moving Idea that he didn't see the woman who was trying to pull her cow out of the river.

"Excuse me," she called out as he passed, "my cow fell into the river. Could you lend me your strength for a moment?"

"Sorry," said the man, "can't stop. Busy." He didn't even glance in her direction.

The Idea remained just out of his reach, but he knew that if he didn't give up he would finally catch it. He just needed to be persistent.

The chase took the man through the valley and over the hills. He was beginning to find it hard to breathe, and this wasn't helped by the cloud of smoke gathering around him. Nearby, a young man was struggling to extinguish a fire in his crops.

"I need help." the young man cried out. "I need to put this fire out or I will lose my harvest this season."

"Sorry," said the man, "can't stop. Busy."

As the cloud of smoke vanished behind him, the sun began to set, and yet the Idea still drifted tantalisingly just out of his reach. But he was gaining on it. He knew that. And just as the sun slipped behind the horizon the man lunged, and was rewarded with the sight of a wild Idea enveloped in his net.

He celebrated. He had caught the Idea! The day's chase had been worth it.

After a few minutes he sat on the ground to catch his breath and rest. He looked at the Idea, sitting neatly in his net. The Idea looked back at him.

"So what happens now?" said the Idea.

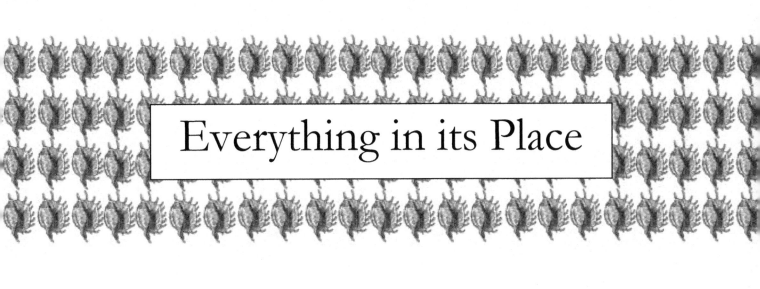

Everything in its Place

*K*nock *knock. Ring ring.*

I opened the door to an energetic young man, who was hopping from foot to foot as though he had pins in his shoes.

"Have you heard? The King is coming! The King is coming!" he said. For one horrible second I thought that he was going to reach in and grab me by my jacket.

"Yes, I had heard something like that," I said.

"Come on then! Come on!" he said, reaching in and grabbing me by my jacket.

"I'll join you later. I have something to do first," I said, sweeping his hand away and shutting the door.

I looked at my list. Item one. The washing up.

So, for about an hour, I happily hummed to myself as I went through the dirty plates and cups and cutlery. By the end, everything was sparkling and back in the kitchen cupboards.

Everything in its place.

I lifted my pen and looked at my list. *Tick.* Washing up done.

Knock knock. Ring ring. Knock knock. Ring ring.

I answered the door. There was a wild-eyed young woman there, her hair frizzy and untamed as though she had recently been electrocuted.

"Have you heard? Do you know? The King is speaking in the marketplace!" she said.

"I suspected that something like that might happen," I said.

"Well, let's go! Quickly!" she said.

"I'll join you later. I really will. I just have something to take care of first," I said, shutting the door and stepping back.

I looked at my list. Item two. Tidying up.

Beds needed to be made. Floors needed to be cleared (health and safety regulations required it). Let me take care of these things first, I thought. I can't leave the house in this state. So I whipped through like a whirlwind, packing away and dusting as I went.

It took me a couple of hours, but I was finally finished.

Everything in its place.

I lifted my pen and looked at my list. *Tick*. Tidying up done.

Knock knock. Ring ring. Knock knock. Ring ring. Knock knock. Ring ring.

This time I found myself facing a stern middle-aged man, his hair turning as grey as his eyes.

"Have you heard? The King is recruiting followers to join him on his quest," he said.

"Really?"

"Come on," he said, holding out a hand.

"Just give me a second," I said, shutting the door.

I looked at my list. The final task. Item three. Paperwork.

I needed to do this. My tax return was due. So I worked hard and quickly, shifting the pile of paper on my desk from the 'In Tray' to the 'Out Tray' as fast as I could manage. Finally my hard work was rewarded. After a few hours, the paperwork was taken care of, and by my calculations I figured I was due a hefty tax refund. A job well done.

Everything in its place.

I lifted my pen and looked at my list. *Tick*. Paperwork done.

Then there was silence.

I made myself a cup of tea, settled down in my favourite armchair and waited for the door to knock and the bell to ring once more.

Nothing. Just silence.

I'm still waiting.

Everything in its place.

The Woman Who Couldn't Keep a Secret

Once upon a time there was a woman who couldn't keep a secret. The people who suffered most were her children, because whenever there was an opportunity to give gifts, whether it was a birthday, or Christmas or some other special occasion, she just couldn't help but excitedly spill the beans to her children, whether they wanted to know or not.

"It's your birthday soon...and you're getting a BRAND NEW BIKE!" she'd say.

"Oh, mum!" her child would say.

"I'm so sorry. I'm so sorry," the mother would say.

"That's OK, mum," the child would sigh.

"You're also getting a BRAND NEW MOBILE PHONE!"

"OH MUM!"

So it would go. The mother, unable to contain her excitement, would blab all to her children, and then feel remorse over the fact that she had – once again – spoiled any sense of surprise that her children might have expected from the special day.

One day, as December approached, she came up with a plan. She had thought of a way to keep herself from revealing those Christmas secrets.

"It's Christmas soon..." she'd say.

Her children would roll their eyes and await the inevitable spoiler, but it didn't come. Their mother would say nothing, and just smile.

The children were astonished.

"Mum, are you feeling all right?"

"Yes, I feel fine," she'd say, smiling.

"Isn't there something you want to tell us?"

"Hmmmm...no, I can't think of anything at the moment," said their mother.

In the run up to Christmas, the children winced every time that their mother opened her mouth, but no secrets were revealed, and by Christmas Eve the children were beginning to believe that their Christmas presents would, for the first time ever, be a delightful mystery.

On Christmas morning, the children spilled down the stairs to the front room, even more excited than they had ever been, and were greeted with the sight of their smiling mother standing by a Christmas tree. Underneath the tree there were no presents at all.

Do you think that the children liked that Christmas any better?

World Views

Many years ago, during the Age of Discovery, three captains set off in order to find a new trade route to the Far East. They gathered round them three crews, like-minded in approach, methods and desire for riches, and once they were ready they set sail.

The first crew looked at their map and said, "This doesn't look like the kind of map we like. Look at the way that the islands and seas are already filled in for you. Where's the freedom in that?" However, the crew found that the other side of the map was blank, and that suited them better, so they turned their map over.

The second crew looked at their map and said, "These countries and so on all look so ridiculous this way. There must be some more pleasing patterns here." They found that by folding their map and turning it a certain way, it made a very pretty arrangement and they decided that this was the map that they would use.

The third crew liked their map the way it was and said, "This is all correct and proper. We can't hope to find the Far East by using anything else, and that's our goal." They left the map the way it was.

After many weeks at sea, the three ships all happened to run aground on the same island.

The first crew consulted their map. It was blank. "Therefore," they concluded, "this so-called island we have crashed into doesn't actually exist." They wandered around the non-existent island, walking into trees that weren't there and ignoring the highly amused natives.

The second crew consulted their map. It had been rearranged. "Therefore," they concluded, "this island we have crashed into is actually the coast of France." They wondered around 'France', commenting on the unusual wildlife and confusing the non-French speaking natives with their attempts to communicate.

The third crew consulted their map. It was accurate. "Therefore," they concluded, "we have arrived at the wrong place." They set about repairing their ship and planning their route to the Far East.

However, the captain of the third crew had a different idea. "I've been giving it some thought and I think we have reached the Far East after all," he told his crew. "There was nothing wrong with the map, and there was nothing wrong with our ship, and our goal was to reach the Far East, so I believe we've made it."

His crew was divided. Some trusted the captain, but others were not convinced. Those who believed the captain berated the rest for their lack of faith in the map and their leader. The rest waved the map angrily and insisted that the captain was in denial. They forgot about repairing the ship, formed two factions and spent their time arguing and rebuking each other.

What with all the stupidity, confusion and arguing, the natives got fed up and left for a different island, abandoning their home to the various groups that had ruined it for them. The island became known as 'La Isla Loca' and every captain worth his salt would take a detour rather than run the risk of having to land there.

All of the crews remained on the island to the end of their days, and they never arrived at the Far East.

Good Stewardship

One day, daddy gave his children some modelling clay. It was a gift. He gave it to them because he loved them. He looked forward to seeing the fruit of their creativity and the smiles on their little faces. Sometimes there is no other agenda.

The children took the modelling clay and thanked daddy and, once he had left the room, they began to play.

When daddy returned to the room he found the children happily creating, as he had hoped. All seemed well, and he was pleased. However, he couldn't help but notice that most of the clay that he had given the children remained unopened on the table. In fact, the children had only opened two colours. He noticed that the boys were working with clay of one colour, blue, and that the girls were working with clay of the other colour, pink.

"Children," said daddy, "why aren't you all using all of the different colours of modelling clay? I didn't give you any such restrictions."

"Silly daddy," said the children. "Everyone knows that blue is for boys and pink is for girls."

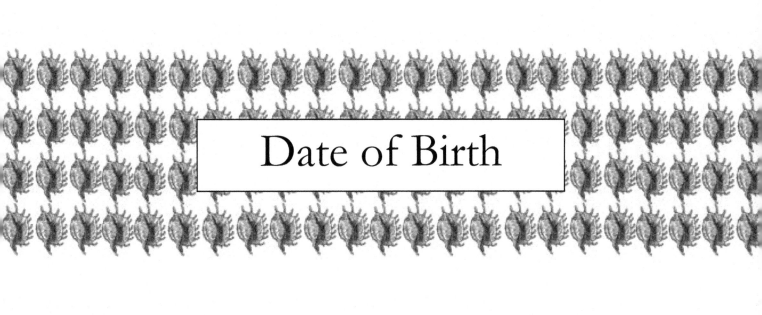

Date of Birth

I remember well the day that I asked the Lord Jesus Christ into my life; the day that I welcomed Him into my heart to forgive my sins.

It was April 19th 1958. I was just a child, but I remember it like it was yesterday. Why wouldn't I? It was the most significant day of my life, the day that shaped its entire direction.

So it was no surprise to me that when I died I was welcomed into heaven. I was surprised, however, to be handed a small slip of paper. At the top of the paper was a large title: DATE THAT I SURRENDERED MY LIFE TO JESUS. Underneath, in bold type, was printed 'April 19th 1958'.

I began to mill around with some of my brothers and sisters, fellow arrivals at our heavenly destination. We clustered together by the gate, waiting to see what would happen next. As we did so, I noticed that the others carried slips of paper like mine, and curiosity got the better of me.

"What does yours say?" I asked one man. He showed me. It had the same heading as mine, DATE THAT I SURRENDERED MY LIFE TO JESUS, and underneath was printed 'June 28th 2006'. He didn't look much younger than me, so I could only assume that I had been a Christian longer than him.

"And yours?" I asked a slim woman who was standing beside me. Again, her paper had the same heading and she had a date on hers too: 'August 2nd 1978'.

As I looked around it seemed to me that, out of all the people there, I had been following Jesus the longest. Now that I was safely through the gates of paradise I allowed myself to feel a little pride. After all, I had served him for so long. I tried to imagine what words of encouragement and praise my Lord would have for me.

Then I saw a man who wasn't carrying a slip of paper. I sidled over to him.

"Pssst." I said. He smiled at me.

"When did you become a Christian?" I said.

"I don't quite remember," he said.

"You don't remember? You don't have a date?"

"I think it was sometime around the winter of 1999, or maybe the following spring. Sometime around there anyway."

"But you've not got one of these, with the date written down?" I showed him my slip of paper. "I became a Christian on April 19th 1958. Look. It's written down. You don't have one of these?" He shook his head.

"No, but I have this." He reached into his coat and pulled out a large rolled-up scroll.

"What's that?"

He unrolled the scroll a little bit so that I could see what it said. At the top of the scroll there was a familiar title: DATE THAT I SURRENDERED MY LIFE TO JESUS. Underneath, in the same bold type, I read the following, 'January 24th 2000', and underneath that, 'February 12th 2000', and underneath that 'February 13th 2000' and underneath that 'February 14th 2000' and underneath that 'February 25th 2000'. And that was just the very top of the scroll. I couldn't begin to imagine how many dates were on the whole thing.

Suddenly, someone yelled. "He's coming!"

A hush descended.

I looked at my piece of paper, and then I looked across at my neighbour's tightly-wrapped scroll, and then I looked back at my piece of paper, and I felt ashamed.

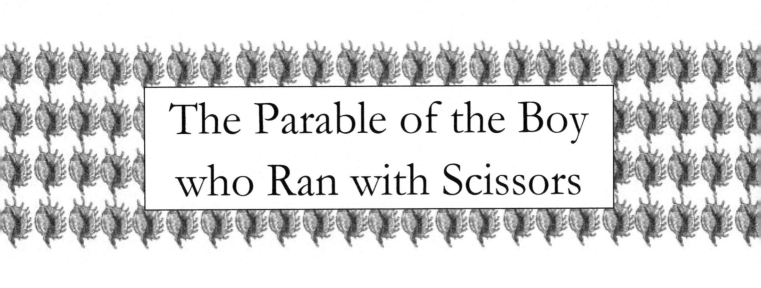

The Parable of the Boy
who Ran with Scissors

There was once a little boy called Ben. Ben was the sort of little boy that always thought that he knew best. You know the type.

"Now Ben, always look both ways before crossing the road," his parents would say. "You must always be aware of the traffic."

"If God wants me to get across the road, then I will get across the road. Checking for traffic shows a lack of faith," Ben would say.

"Now Ben, don't go into the woods alone. The woods are full of all kinds of dangerous beasties like wolves and bears and goblins."

"It sounds like you want me to be afraid of the woods. The Bible says that perfect love drives out all fear, so I'll go into the woods if I want to," said Ben.

"Now Ben, never visit the city of Mammon. There are one hundred traps and temptations waiting for the naive young tourist."

"But there are people there who need to hear about the love of our Lord Jesus Christ. If I want to go to Mammon, then I'll go to Mammon," said Ben, mesmerised by the bright lights and driving beat of the city.

Poor little Ben. He didn't stand a chance.

None so Blind

Life was very difficult, living in the darkness. It made even the simplest tasks so very hard. The only consolation you had was in knowing that you weren't alone. Everyone around you was struggling in the dark too, unable to see.

Brian had quite a good routine, and usually managed to get through the day without too many problems. He would wake up, get up and get dressed – no problems there – and then he would have breakfast, get ready for the day and go to work. He would occasionally scald himself while making a cup of tea, or trip over the doorstep when he was leaving for work, but on the whole his life was pretty well under control. He knew that there were others who were struggling more than him, and he was thankful for what he had.

After a hard day's work he would come home and relax in front of the television (though he never had any idea what he was watching). On Sundays he would go to church. He enjoyed that very much. It was a great time to catch up with friends, but more than that, it was the time in his schedule when he connected with God. He found it extremely helpful in the face of another week. He would sing songs to worship God (and he really meant it all, in his heart. He really did). He would listen to teaching about God and find ways to apply it to his life. One of the most encouraging things for him was when the preacher would stand up and describe what it was going to be like when they went to heaven. In heaven, he said, they would all be able to see. The Bible told them that there would be no more darkness. The preacher would talk about all the different shapes and colours that there would be. It was always so exciting to hear about it, and Brian liked to think about it a lot. It gave him something to look forward to, because he knew that one day, after he died and went to heaven, he wouldn't have to live in darkness any more. He really, really looked forward to that day, because although he had quite a happy life, he knew that – deep down – this wasn't how it was supposed to be.

One of the most incredible things about Brian's church was that there were a few people there who claimed that they were already able to see. Most of the people in his church dismissed these claims. "They can't really see," they said, "they're just saying that." Of course, there was no real way to know. You had to take their word for it – or not. Brian had asked the preacher about them once, and he had agreed with most of the congregation. They couldn't see – the Bible told us that we were still in darkness, and that we had to wait until the end before we could see. Those who claimed that they could see now were, well, they were either mistaken or, worse, deceitful. But they were tolerated as long as they didn't cause too much trouble. After all, church was supposed to be a welcoming, friendly place that was open to all.

But Brian was cursed with an active imagination, and he couldn't help but wonder what it would be like to be able to see now. He would listen to the preacher, and hear the beautiful things that he would talk about, and he would sometimes just daydream about what it would be like, and that is how he and Kirby got talking.

Kirby was one of the people in his church who claimed that he could see. Most of the people in the church seemed to think that Kirby was harmless, but a little bit wrong. Brian got the impression that most people felt sorry for him, but Brian found what Kirby had to say very interesting, and a little bit inspiring.

Over many weeks they met for coffee on Saturday mornings, and Brian would ask Kirby to tell him what the world looked like, in all its glorious colours and contours. It wasn't long, however, before Kirby began trying to convince Brian that it was quite possible for him to see the colours and shapes for himself, that he didn't have to rely on Kirby's descriptions, that he could experience it all first hand. Brian was scared by what Kirby was suggesting. It seemed to be at odds with what he had heard in his church over the years and, not only that, it seemed to be at odds with his own experience. After all, if it was possible for him to see, if it was really that easy, wouldn't he have done it by now? Kirby explained that actually it was quite easy to remove the darkness, but it wasn't easy at all – not one little bit – to live as a seeing man amongst the blind.

Brian couldn't sleep that night, thinking about the things that Kirby had said. There was a voice inside him that argued loudly against Kirby's claims. Kirby was wrong.

Things were okay as they were, weren't they? It wasn't too bad. Kirby was an idealist, mistaken and unrealistic. Dangerous even. No. Don't listen to him. Don't complicate things.

But there was another voice. A voice buried deeper within, that could be quite loud when Brian let it. A voice that asked "What If...?" A voice that stirred a feeling that just couldn't believe that what he had now was as good as it got.

Night after night, Brian lay awake, in turmoil, agonising and wrestling. Then one night, suddenly and out of nowhere, he made a decision. And then he slept a deep and refreshing sleep.

The next Saturday morning, Brian told Kirby that he was ready to know the truth. Kirby asked him if he'd ever touched his own eyes. Brian couldn't recall whether or not he had. Kirby asked him to touch his eyes now. Brian gently lifted his hands up and felt his face. When he got to his eyes, he felt the soft sensation of cloth under his fingertips. Kirby explained that it was a blindfold, and that he should take it off. Brian hesitated for a few moments, lingering on the edge before his desire pushed him over.

The colours! The brightness! The joy!

Brian could hardly contain himself. After all these years living in the darkness, if only he'd known that it was as simple as removing his blindfold. The world seemed like a totally different place now. He found himself noticing things that he'd been totally oblivious to before, but already he began to understand what Kirby had meant about being a seeing man amongst the blind. When you're oblivious to something you don't spend any time wondering about it, or feeling responsible for it. It was different now.

Church was a new experience the following morning. He saw all his friends, the ones he had known for years, and immediately realised how foolish everyone looked, stumbling around with their blindfolds on. He spoke freely with Kirby, and those who had no blindfolds, but he found it a bit difficult to carry on with the others as though nothing had changed. He noticed that some of those who had claimed that they could see were still blindfolded, and he saw others, including the preacher, who had drawn crude eyes on their blindfolds.

When Brian tried to talk to his friends about his new sight, they reacted in a variety of ways. Some sounded like they were interested, but Brian could see the grimace on their questioning faces. Others reacted with cool suspicion. He sat through the sermon, but all the old words that used to inspire him seemed so empty now that he knew the truth.

Bittersweet. That was the word that Brian would use.

Wings

The boy was a little different. He had been born with wings, tiny little buds just below his shoulder blades. It's not easy being different, even if that being different is to have wings. But we're all different really, aren't we? That's a good thing. It's probably why we're all so understanding of one another and the struggles that we face.

At first, some people were not sure what to make of the boy, but as he grew so did his wings, and people began to be curious and even jealous. After all, there are ways of being different that seem exciting and fascinating to others, and having wings was certainly a unique way of being different.

One day, the boy asked God a question. "Why did you give me wings, God?"

"So that you can make others happy," said God.

The boy pondered this. He made friends easily, and nothing made him happier than seeing them happy, and it troubled him greatly whenever one of his friends was sad. But the boy found that he was able to help his friends become happy again. All he needed to do was to reach around and pluck one of the brightly coloured feathers from his wings, and then he would use the feather to tickle his friend until the tears had been replaced by laughter.

The boy had many friends, and his wings made many people happy, but there were only a limited number of feathers and soon his wings were nothing more than stumps.

One day God said to the boy, "Where are the wings that I gave you?"

"I have given them away to make my friends happy," said the boy.

"How happy your friends would have been, even the whole world, if you had shown them what it was like to fly," said God.

Mister Thigh

No-one knew his real name. Everyone knew him as 'Mister Thigh' and, right now, Mister Thigh stood on the trail like a human roadblock. He was able to do this because he was probably the biggest man that you have ever seen, and he wanted to do this because he also happened to be the meanest man that you have ever seen. This part of the road was the perfect place to be if you wanted to bully and steal from travellers, being just beyond a corner so that your intended victim would not see you until it was too late. Mister Thigh's method this day was slightly more subtle than simply demanding valuables. Instead he would make an offer that the traveller would find very hard to refuse, and his terrifying and utterly deserved reputation would do the rest.

Mister Thigh smiled to himself as he heard the clip clop of a horse's hooves coming round the corner, and he hefted the stout branch that he had pulled from a tree at the side of the road. Almost immediately an elderly man on a horse trotted into view. Mister Thigh noted, with undisguised greed, the two hefty money bags hanging from the horse's saddle.

"Hello there sir. Fine day, isn't it?" Mister Thigh feigned a respectful bow.

The elderly rider pulled his horse to a stop, went pale and gulped. "H...h...hello there, Mis...mister Thigh," he said.

Mister Thigh smiled, revealing two rows of perfect, gleaming, pointed teeth.

"Can I interest you in this fine stick? I think it's magical." Mister Thigh waved the tree branch in what can only be described as a menacing way.

"W...w...why not? How much?" the old man said, well aware on which side his bread was buttered.

Mister Thigh was big and strong, but that didn't mean that he was stupid. On the contrary, he had a finely tuned brain ticking in his head. He quickly sized up the money bags, and made an estimate.

"Well, I'd let this go for two hundred coins, even though it's worth much more."

"But...but that's all the money I have," the old man said, regretting the words as soon as they had left his mouth.

Mister Thigh was pleased with his accurate guess. "Well, it's your lucky day then, isn't it?"

The old man rode on, penniless but with a newly-acquired tree branch, and he considered himself lucky. Everyone who knew Mister Thigh would agree that he had been lucky indeed.

Mister Thigh barely had time to collect a new branch from the side of the road before he heard someone else approaching. This time the horse's hooves were accompanied by a rattling squeak. Mister Thigh, connoisseur of transportation, recognised the sound of a horse-drawn cart, and indeed round the corner came a merchant riding just that.

"Well met, traveller. Isn't it a nice day?" Mister Thigh smiled.

As the cart trickled to a halt, the merchant went pale and gulped.

"Uhhhh...Mister Thigh. What a surprise to meet you on the road."

"A fortunate surprise for you, sir. I am looking to trade this magical stick, and I feel like it could be your lucky day." Mister Thigh swung the branch like a lumberjack.

"How kind," said the merchant, "but I...I don't think I need a magic stick at the moment."

Mister Thigh raised an eyebrow. "Really? Wouldn't you like to know what magic the stick possesses? You may change your mind."

"Um, very well."

"I am fairly certain," continued Mister Thigh, "that the magical properties that this branch possesses would render its owner immune to sudden and unfortunate head injuries. And that's just for starters."

"On second thoughts, I believe that I might be interested in such a trade, but I'm not sure I have anything that would match the value of this clearly unique stick."

Mister Thigh looked to be deep in thought, but in reality he was utilising his finely-trained nose.

"Hmmmm, though it's hardly fair on myself, I think I would be willing to trade this stick for, say, a cart full of exotic and rare spices," he said after a moment. The merchant looked crestfallen.

The merchant rode on, without his cart, but clutching a twisted piece of wood, and he considered himself fortunate indeed. He knew that there were many who had encountered Mister Thigh and not escaped with their lives.

As Mister Thigh ripped a third limb from the nearby tree, his ears detected the sound of shuffling feet approaching the corner. The third victim in as many minutes. It was turning out to be a fine day indeed, but the predatory smile slipped from his lips as he saw his next victim. It was a small boy, dressed in rags, tossing a ball into the air and catching it again as it fell.

The reason for the change in Mister Thigh's mood was because he had a long memory, and the sight of the child brought an unsavoury thought to his mind. He was remembering something that had happened a long time ago, the time when he had burnt the Witch's Cottage to the ground, while she was still inside. He had never told anyone, for to do so would have been an unforgivable sign of weakness, but sometimes, sometimes in the darkest, loneliest part of the night he could still hear the raspy-voiced prophecy that she had called out from her fiery tomb:

"The child will be your undoing! The child will be your undoing!"

A horrible memory. A chill had weaved its way down his spine as the scruffy urchin walked into view. But he was Mister Thigh, and he recovered his poise almost instantly. And as the child moved closer, Mister Thigh found himself gazing at the ball that was being thrown up and down. The sun glinted off it in such a way that Mister Thigh found himself salivating involuntarily. It was no ball. It was a pearl; the largest pearl Mister Thigh had ever seen in his life. Any last doubts were elbowed aside by greed.

"Hello there, boy. That's a fine looking ball that you have there," he said, tapping the ground with the stout branch.

The boy slowed to a halt, looked at Mister Thigh and shrugged.

"Push off, mister," he said.

Mister Thigh was thrown. Did this foolish child not know to whom he spoke? Well, he would certainly know after this. Without taking his eyes off the pearl, Mister Thigh ploughed on.

"Would you like to trade your ball for this fine, magical stick, young man? Think of all the adventures you might have with such an amazing item at your side."

"I said, 'Push off'. Are you deaf as well as ugly?" the child said.

No-one still living had ever spoken to Mister Thigh this way. This boy would pay, oh yes. All pretence was now gone.

"Give me that pearl," he snarled, hefting the branch over his shoulder, "or I'll stove your head in with this club."

"You want my ball? Why didn't you say so?"

The boy swung his arm back and threw the pearl at Mister Thigh as hard as he could. It sailed through the air, crashed against the surprised Mister Thigh's forehead and sent him sprawling to the ground, dead.

73

The Worst Crime

One of the new president's first acts was to pass a law abolishing slavery. He entrusted two of his faithful heralds with sharing this news around the city.

The first herald came upon a group of slaves and could barely contain his excitement.

"Guess what!" he cried, grabbing one slave by the shoulders. "Great news! You've been freed! The new president has revoked the law of the last president. He thinks slavery is evil and has abolished it! You're all free! Free!"

And amongst this group of slaves there was much dancing and much rejoicing.

The second herald came upon a group of slaves and called them to order.

"I have some great news for you. I have here a new law. Listen while I read it. Ahem. Part One. Slavery as defined by the constitution. Part One, Section 1A. Legal definitions of slavery. For the purpose of this legal document slavery will be defined as the following..."

And amongst this group of slaves there was much sleeping and much boredom.

Big Dreams

I knew a young man who had been captured by a Big Dream. His eyes sparkled with life and his voice quivered with passion. The Big Dream was all that he could talk about. It was both inspiring and a bit annoying. It was a lot like being around someone who was in love.

I saw him again a few months later. He still glowed and talked about the Big Dream, but he seemed different. I stared at him for a couple of minutes before I realised what it was. He was thinner. No, that's the wrong word. He was flatter. Yes, that's it. Flatter. Not metaphorically, you understand. Actually flatter, like a sandwich that someone had scraped the filling out of.

The third time I saw him was about a year after that. He still talked about the Big Dream, but he seemed uncertain. Sadder somehow. But that wasn't really what you noticed. You saw it straight away. There was no depth to him. Literally. He was paper-thin. Two dimensional. Like a cartoon character after a boulder had fallen on him. But he still wouldn't shut up about that Big Dream.

Here's the thing. Dream a Big Dream if you want to, but if all you do is dream, eventually the weight of it will crush you.

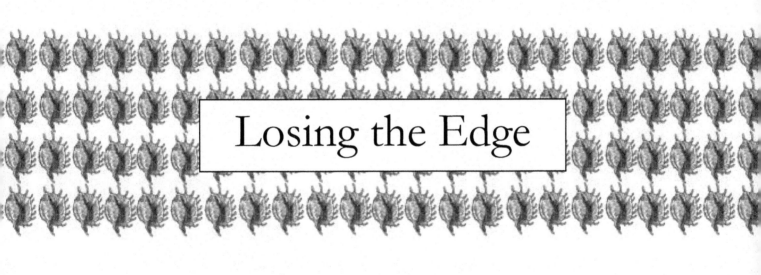

Losing the Edge

It's a cruel world, the stone thought to itself. It sat here, by the water, day after day, with the island in sight but well beyond its reach. There was no way across the water, and nothing to be done but sit there with its stone brothers and stone sisters and dream of what could be.

Sometimes, someone would come along, pick up one of the stone brothers or stone sisters and try to hurl it across to the island. Every time this happened there was a moment of excitement. Perhaps this one would succeed. Perhaps this time, one of the stones would make it to the island. They hoped and waited, but every time they were disappointed. The stone would be thrown, with all the strength that the thrower possessed, but would fall short every time. Without fail, there would be a plop as the stone hit the water and sank beneath the surface forever.

A cruel world indeed. The stone had given up all hope. It knew that it would never make it to the island. None of them ever had. But what if someone came along and tried to throw it? It didn't know what waited beneath the water, so it was afraid. It would rather sit here and live with its disappointment. Rather that than be thrown into the deep blue unknown. So the stone grew a collection of jagged angles and sharp edges. No-one would pick it up now. It was too dangerous.

One day, a man came along and looked through the rocks gathered by the water's edge. The stone waited to see what would happen and, with mounting horror, began to realise that the man was going to pick it up.

No, it thought, I don't want to be thrown into the water! Sure enough, the man reached down and grabbed the stone. The stone struggled against the hand gathered around it, and with satisfaction felt its sharp edges dig into the man's flesh. Blood began to flow.

But to its surprise, the stone was not thrown – either to the ground or into the water. Rather it was placed into the man's pocket and taken home. Once there, the man removed the stone from his pocket and set to work.

He hacked at the stone with tools and rubbed it with a rough cloth. The stone begged the man to stop, because the work he was doing was painful to it, but the man ignored the stone and carried on.

Please, the stone begged, it hurts. But the man carried on with his task.

Please, the stone begged, my edges are a part of me. But the man carried on with his task.

Please, the stone begged, they protect me. But the man carried on with his task.

After some time the man finally finished his work, and put the stone back into his pocket. Then he walked back to the water's edge, carrying the now-smooth stone with him. Then he pulled it out of his pocket, and swung his arm back to throw.

Please, the stone begged, don't throw me, I don't want to go into the water. I'm sorry I hurt you. But it was too late. The man followed through and the stone felt itself soaring through the air. It braced itself for impact with the water and then CRUNCH! It smacked into the water, but something strange happened. The stone didn't sink. Instead, it spun off the water's surface and leapt into the air again.

What's going on? thought the stone.

Then, suddenly, it hit the water once more, but again it bounced up into the air and continued its journey. A third time the stone skimmed off the water, and flew through the air like a bird.

Then, SMACK! The stone hit again, but it wasn't water this time. It was dry land. The stone gathered its thoughts and took in its surroundings. It was on the island! Somehow, the man had thrown him all the way from the water's edge to the island he had believed it impossible to reach.

The stone looked back across the water, and saw the man. It watched as the man waved his goodbye, and then it smiled to itself as the man bent down to pick up another stone.

Happily Ever After

Worshipped and adored by a congregation that was captivated by his charisma and enthralled by his sermons, his church just kept growing and growing. He led a church of hundreds, but he couldn't lead himself. As we all know, secrets have a habit of breaking free.

"Was it really true?" they said. The great man brought low by a stressful year and a woman he met in a bar? His family wrecked, his congregation heartbroken, and the man himself totally ruined.

He appeared in the pulpit, eyes full of tears, to confess and renounce; to apologise and ask for forgiveness. Well, God can redeem and God can bring beautiful things out of terrible mess. Who are we to cast the first stone?

And who was to blame, really? We pushed him so hard and expected so much, and I hear that his wife is quite a difficult woman behind closed doors. He was a great man, but he was – after all – just a man. And it takes two to tango, doesn't it? What kind of a woman throws herself at a married man in a bar? There's a word for a woman like that. Several words, actually. We understand. He was only human.

We believe in forgiveness. We believe in grace. Did you see him there, weeping in the pulpit? What humility! What courage! It brought tears to my eyes.

His preaching has been ever better since then, don't you think? Just goes to show, doesn't it? And his new book is selling quite well, I hear. Hallelujah. Three cheers for redemption and another happy ending.

But endings are never quite that simple, are they?

All that weeping, but who wept for God's honour, dirt smeared on His face once more? Who wept for the woman in the bar, sold into slavery because she'd never been told that she was worth something? And when she died of a drug overdose a year later, who, other than the Holy Spirit, wept at her funeral?

People would rather have a happy ending than the right ending.

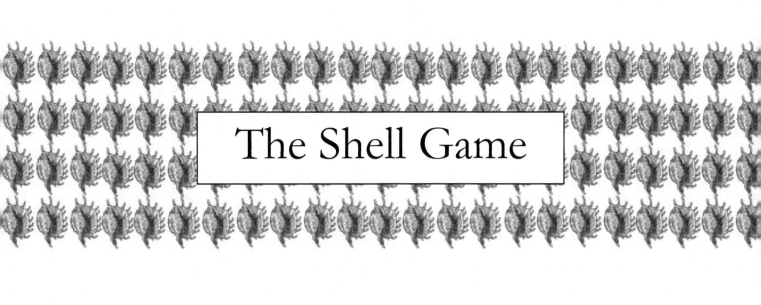

The Shell Game

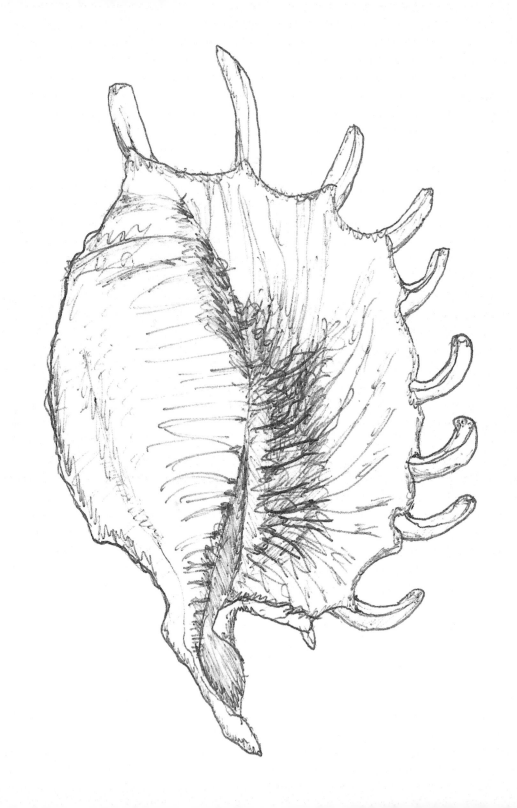

I was walking down the street and I saw a man with a stall set up by the side of the road. He had three cups on a table, and he would put something under one of the cups and then switch them all around a few times. You know the kind of thing that I mean. He was charging £5 for people to try and guess which cup the object was under.

I watched him do it a few times. No-one won – they always picked the wrong cup – but I was curious. For one thing, I couldn't see what he kept hiding under the cup.

Some more people came up, paid their money and tried to win. He managed to outsmart them every time and they never guessed the right cup. I wondered what was so appealing about playing the game, so I stopped someone who was coming away and asked him why he had played.

"Because if you pick the right cup, you get to keep the object that he's hidden under there."

"What's under the cup?" I said.

"Happiness," said the man, before walking on.

Well, I watched him for a few more minutes until I thought I'd figured out how he was doing it, and then I decided that I'd give it a try. £5 for Happiness seemed like a very good deal, so I figured it was worth the risk.

I gave him £5 and very carefully watched him switch the cups around. I decided that the Happiness must be under the middle one, but it wasn't. So I paid another £5 to try again. I watched him more cloesly this time, and was sure that it was under the left cup, but this time it was under the middle one. I tried again, and again, and again, but I didn't manage to guess correctly. Not even once.

I walked away, disappointed but not surprised.

Further down the road, on the street corner, was a man. He stood there, offering something to people as they walked past.

"Take one. It's free," he said to me, holding out an object.

"What is it?"

"Happiness," he said.

"What's the catch?"

"There isn't one," he said.

"That guy over there was charging £5 for a chance at Happiness, and you're just offering it to me for free?"

"That's right," said the man.

"It's a trick."

"No, it's not," he said.

"No, you won't get me. I'm not falling for that," I said, and stepped away.

I watched the man for a while, holding out Happiness to anyone who walked by, but no-one took what he offered. Like me, they were suspicious. Why was he doing it? And why would he offer something valuable for nothing? The guy with the stall had the right idea, I thought. But this guy on the corner, what does he think he's doing? Doesn't he understand how people think?

Of Myself and Others

There I was, and I knew I wasn't good enough. My friends were so much better, so much more gifted. Petra was so good at caring for and loving others. Alice was a fantastically gifted writer. Thomas had the ability to teach and communicate so clearly. Simon seemed to walk so closely with God and have such a strong relationship with Him. I wanted to be just like them, to do and say all the things that they did and said.

I went to visit the Wise Man. I knew he would be able to help. "How can I be like the others?" I asked him.

"You should go and speak to them, and ask them to show you the way," he replied.

So I went first to Petra and asked her how I could be like her. She told me that I needed to feel the agonies of others and put their needs before mine, that I needed to make a discipline of loving. So I tried to do what she asked, but I found myself tired and bruised and I wasn't any different. In fact, I suspected that I was even worse off. So I went back to the Wise Man.

"I don't think that worked. How can I become like the others?"

"Don't give up. Go and speak to them and ask them to show you the way."

So I went next to Alice and asked her how I could be like her. She told me that I needed to make a habit of writing and playing with language, that I needed to see the story in everything and try to capture it. So I tried what she asked, but I found myself confused and losing my love for words and I wasn't any different. In fact, I was pretty sure that I was even worse off. So I went back to the Wise Man.

"That definitely didn't work. Look, how can I become like the others?"

"Hmmmm. I still think that you should go and speak to them and ask them to show you the way."

So I went next to Thomas and asked him how I could be like him. He told me that I needed to truly understand my subject, that I needed to perfect my attention to detail. So I tried what he asked, but I found myself becoming more insecure about my ability and overwhelmed by my ignorance and I wasn't any different. In fact, I was sure that I was worse off. So I went back to the Wise Man.

"I thought you were supposed to be wise. It's a simple question. How can I become like the others?"

"OK, try one more time. Go and speak to them and ask them to show you the way."

So I went next to Simon and asked him how I could be like him. He told me that I needed to forge my love for God in the fires of discipline and be content with asking questions that were never answered, that I needed to focus on being rather than doing. So I tried what he asked, but I found myself bored and depressed and I wasn't any different. In fact, I knew with certainty that I was worse off. So I went back to the Wise Man.

"I don't know what you're playing at, but this hasn't worked at all. I'm tired and hurt and lost and depressed. It's too hard to copy the others. What's wrong with just being me?"

"Ah," said the Wise Man. "Now we're getting somewhere."

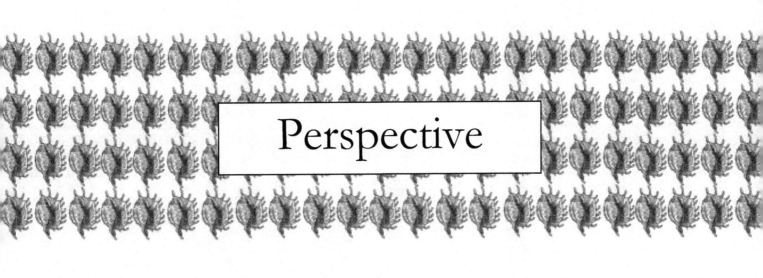

Perspective

"Yachal, come with me. I have something to show you," said the Lord.

The angel looked nervously over his shoulder. "Me, Lord?" he said.

"Yes. Come on. I want you to see this." The Lord beckoned Yachal over. "Look down there," He said, pointing to Earth.

Yachal peered down through the mist and saw a church service in full swing. The congregation were gathered and being led in worship by an older gentleman. Their singing lifted up to heaven like sweet incense. Their faces reflected the celestial glory, their orchestral voices lifted in praise. They practically glowed with holiness. In fact, they shone like...well, like angels, thought Yachal. All they needed were the halos, and Yachal wasn't too sure he didn't see a few of those scattered about. He could watch this all day.

"Keep watching," said the Lord.

Suddenly the mist gathered again, and dispersed once more. This time Yachal saw the same place later in the day. This was the evening service, and the congregation was, this time, being led by a younger man. Immediately, Yachal noticed that this was an entirely different gathering. As heavenly as the first group were, this lot were the complete opposite. Their worship didn't float up as sweet incense, but rather sank into the ground like something a lot less fragrant. This congregation seemed to be made up of denizens of the lowest depths of hell. Their harsh, gritty voices were murdering the songs. Yachal swore that he could see some horns and forked tails amongst the crowd.

The Lord saw his grimace and said, "What do you make of that then? What's the difference?"

"Is this a test?"

"Yachal, everything is a test," the Lord said.

"Well, it's obvious," said the angel. "What you have here is one of those churches where the two different services are attended by totally different congregations. The morning service is attended by the saintly members of the church, while the evening is attended by the...other ones."

"No. Try again," said the Lord.

"Hmmmmm. Maybe it's not the same church after all. Maybe it's two totally different churches with identical buildi-"

"Way off. Have another go," said the Lord.

"Aha, I've got it!" Yachal snapped his fingers. "It's about the men leading the congregations! The one in the morning delivers a message that appeals to those who are already comfortable in their faith and the one in the evening preaches in a way that draws the lost and the wayward to him."

"Close, but no. Would you like a clue?" said the Lord, a faint smile on His face.

"Yes please, Lord," said Yachal.

"OK. It's exactly the same congregation in both services."

"What? How is that possible?" the angel said.

"I told you that your third guess was close," said the Lord. "Watch this."

The mist rolled in and dispersed once more. This time Yachal saw a couple sitting down at the breakfast table in a home that looked comfortable and welcoming. Immediately he recognised one of the two as the older man who had been leading the first service. Yachal listened as he and his wife talked freely about how things were going in the church. He spoke about the congregation with warmth and hope. He spoke about its strengths and the vision he had for individual members.

He shared with his wife his dreams, the things of heaven that he could see in each one of them, their potential and what they could become. Yachal could not help but be moved by such a warm example of love.

The mist gathered and faded out one final time. Now Yachal was watching a very similar scene to the one he had just witnessed, but this time the couple sitting at the breakfast table included the younger man who had been leading the evening service. He was talking to his wife about how things were in the church, but from his perspective as the assistant to the older man. His words were just as passionate, but they were far from complimentary. He complained about the congregation; he labelled it stubborn and stupid. He talked about how members of the church seemed unable to grasp what he was trying to do. He listed the sins of the people: a lack of enthusiasm, a lack of vision and a fatal lack of spiritual vitality. He saw no strength or potential in them, only the hardness of their hearts and their failures. As he listened, Yachal's ears began to hurt.

This second picture faded out, and the Lord smiled at the angel.

"Do you understand now?"

"Yes, Lord, I think so," said Yachal.

"Yes. I rather think that you do," said the Lord.

Butterfly

How wonderful it was to be a butterfly, flitting from flower to flower and drinking nectar, wowing the crowds with beautiful bright wings, floating in the air, enjoying the breeze. What a fantastic life.

This particular butterfly was enjoying all the privileges of its species, and pondering as it flew. It liked to reflect while it meandered from petal to petal, thinking through this and that. Today it was reminiscing.

"Remember when I used to be a caterpillar?" it said to itself. "It's so much better being a butterfly, being able to fly and being so admired. Yes, I'm much happier now."

The butterfly landed on a bright yellow petal.

"But I did enjoy eating leaves. Yes, they could be quite tasty," it said, as it sucked up a little nectar. "Yes, leaves," it continued the thought. "I'm not complaining about being a butterfly, but nectar gets a little...samey after a while. It's nectar, nectar, nectar every day. When I was a caterpillar I could try different leaves and plants whenever I liked. It seemed like a much more varied diet."

The butterfly hopped into the air and floated in the breeze.

"Flying is fun, I'll admit that," the butterfly said to itself, "but there is something to be said for walking. Of course, it was slower and more complicated and I never saw the sky or the sun, but still...it wasn't a bad way to travel."

The butterfly settled on another petal.

"I liked my legs. I had so many of them. Oh, travelling along on so many legs was satisfying. It was so hard to keep them coordinated that I got a real sense of achievement whenever I managed to actually get somewhere. It took real skill, you know. I don't mind flying. It's certainly easier. But I like a challenge every now and then."

The butterfly sighed.

"Maybe," it wondered, "I could go back. Do you think I could go back, just for a little while? What harm would it do? Just for a little while. To try eating leaves again. To walk around instead of flying around. I think it would be good for me. It would help me remember where I came from. I could make contact with some of my old caterpillar friends. Yes. I think it would be a good thing."

The butterfly, its mind made up, settled in the undergrowth on the green stem of a flower.

"It's all coming back to me," it said. "I remember! Why did I ever leave? Why did I ever turn my back on my caterpillar ways? I was so happy! I'm so thankful for this second chance!"

But the butterfly was not as thankful as the frog, who had just seen bright colourful wings come to a halt on a very plain green stem, well within his jumping range. Butterfly or caterpillar, it was all the same to him.

"Ribbit," the frog said, "time for lunch!"

Harder than it Looks

The old woman's name was Vera. It was an old name, but it suited her. Well, of course it did, because she was an old woman. An old name for an old woman.

Vera was one of those old women who had always been around. No-one could remember a time when she hadn't been there. But that didn't mean much to the other townsfolk. Being around for a long time was just a fact. It didn't mean that they owed her anything. What it did mean was that everyone knew her, and therefore everyone had an opinion about her.

She was not very popular, for example, with the members of the recently formed Rabbit Protection League. When they gathered for their meetings, there was always time for them to complain about Vera, even though she was never on the official agenda. Old and familiar she may be, but she was also Public Enemy Number One and held up as an example of exactly the very thing the League had been set up to campaign against.

Why was this? What could an admittedly small but very determined group of animal lovers have against an old woman who was sometimes seen buying new clothes but never seen wearing them?

It was as simple as this. Vera, old dear that she was, had a lucky rabbit's foot and wherever she went, her foot went with her, very prominently displayed. You couldn't miss it, at least not if you were the sort of person who cared whether or not other people carried dead animal limbs around with them.

"I saw her in the market again! Disgraceful!"

"Someone should do something! It should be illegal!"

"Rabbits have rights too! Did the rabbit surrender its foot of its own free will? I think not!"

Vera knew that the Rabbit Protection League thought that she was violent and deranged, but she didn't care. The rest of the town also knew what the Rabbit Protection League thought, and they also knew that Vera didn't care, and this made some of them a little curious, especially a little girl called Olive.

No-one was quite sure if Olive was a suitable name for a little girl. Some people in the town thought that it was an old name, like Vera, and should be attached to an old woman. Others thought that it suited a young girl just fine, and left it at that. All of this is very interesting, but not really relevant to Olive, Vera, the Rabbit Protection League or our story. I just thought that I'd mention it.

Anyway, one day, Olive skipped up to Vera, who greeted her warmly.

"Vera," said Olive, "I was wondering about somet-"

"Wondering, eh? A very healthy habit in a young girl, I must say," said Vera.

"Why do you show off that rabbit's foot? You know it annoys the Rabbit Protection League. Why don't you just keep it hidden away? You'd save yourself a lot of trouble, and it would probably shorten their meetings by at least half an hour."

"Dear child," said Vera, "why should I hide something that reminds me who I am?"

Olive wasn't very satisfied with this answer, and it seemed like Vera was just looking for trouble, but she let it go. She wanted to ask her second question.

You see, the Rabbit Protection League weren't the only ones who liked to talk about Vera. She was also a topic of conversation for the newly formed group Philosophers and Thinkers Rallied Opposite Naive, Ignorant, Superstitious Expression (known as PATRONISE for short). Whereas the Rabbit Protection League regarded Vera as Public Enemy Number One, PATRONISE viewed her with head-shaking pity and contempt.

Now what could this group have against a little old lady who was often seen buying food in the marketplace, but rarely seen taking it home with her?

Well, they didn't like her lucky rabbit's foot either.

"Look at the poor old dear with her lucky rabbit's foot. She's probably half-senile already. She'll be wearing her underpants on her head next."

"She's a shining example of the old ways. Thankfully, humanity has evolved past her primitive and outdated superstitious thinking."

"Now now, ladies and gentlemen. We should pity her. Some people are just weak minded. The truth is too much for them. They're just too weak to get through life without a crutch."

Now, Vera knew that PATRONISE regarded her as some deluded relic of the past, but she didn't care about that either. That also intrigued little Olive.

"I have another question, Vera," she said.

"Ask away, dear," Vera said.

"Isn't it all a bit ridiculous anyway? To be carrying around a lucky rabbit's foot in this day and age?"

"Lucky?" Vera said, her brow creased with confusion. "I don't remember ever claiming that it was lucky."

Well, before Olive could respond to this strange comment, Vera was off, bustling through the crowd. Olive decided that the only way to make sense of this strange old lady was to follow her and see what she got up to, so that is what she did.

Olive could barely keep up. It was almost as if the wizened old dear was on roller skates. But Olive did keep up, and she saw some amazing things. She saw Vera visiting the sick at the hospital. She saw Vera bringing food and clothes to the orphanage. She saw Vera reading stories to the children in a grim part of town. She saw Vera doing all kinds of good deeds and thoughtful things for people. Olive realised that she'd never thought about it before; about why the orphans always seemed to have plenty of food and clothes; about why the sick people in the hospital seemed at peace and cared for. She'd never realised that Vera was behind it all. She'd always thought it just happened. But now she knew.

"Vera," said Olive one day, when the old lady had stopped to catch her breath for a moment.

"Yes, dear?" Vera replied.

"Why do you do it? Why do you do everything that you do?"

"I have to, dear," Vera said.

"You have to?"

"Yes," Vera said, "I have to do what the rabbit's foot tells me to do." The old lady winked at the little girl, and she was off again.

She had to do what the rabbit's foot told her to do? What kind of life philosophy was that? Perhaps the Rabbit Protection League and PATRONISE were right. Perhaps she was just a batty old lady after all.

A few years passed. Olive grew up a little bit, and Vera died. Her funeral was attended by the poor, the sick and the orphans, and by Olive. No-one from the Rabbit Protection League or PATRONISE was there, and why should they be?

After the funeral, curiosity slowly pulled Olive towards Vera's house, which was tucked away on the outskirts of town. As she walked along the streets, she thought about Vera. A crazy old lady she may have been, but the world would be a poorer place without her.

"I suppose," she muttered to herself, "that if I wanted to be like someone, then I could do a lot worse than being like Vera."

Olive arrived at Vera's house and tried the front door. It was unlocked. She let herself in, because that's the kind of thing that girls like Olive do. Vera's house was plain and tidy, which is exactly what Olive expected. There was hardly any furniture, but it still felt like a cosy home. In the dining room, Olive was surprised to find a sturdy wooden table. Well, she wasn't really surprised to find the table. That was a very normal and therefore unsurprising thing to find in a dining room. What had surprised her was the large envelope sitting on top of the table. It had surprised her because written on it, in large letters that you could see from the moment that you entered the room, were two words: 'For Olive.'

If Olive had ever read Alice's Adventures in Wonderland then this is the point at which she would have said, "Curiouser and curiouser". But she hadn't, so she didn't.

She simply picked up the envelope and shook it. Nothing happened, so she opened it. Out, into her outstretched hand, fell Vera's rabbit's foot. What did this mean? What was Vera thinking? What was going on? Olive stood there for a little while, stunned. Then she gave voice to her confusion.

"What am I supposed to do now?" she said out loud.

Then the rabbit's foot spoke to her.

It said, "Feed the poor, heal the sick, love the unlovable, preach the good news and set the captives free."

And Olive finally understood.

118

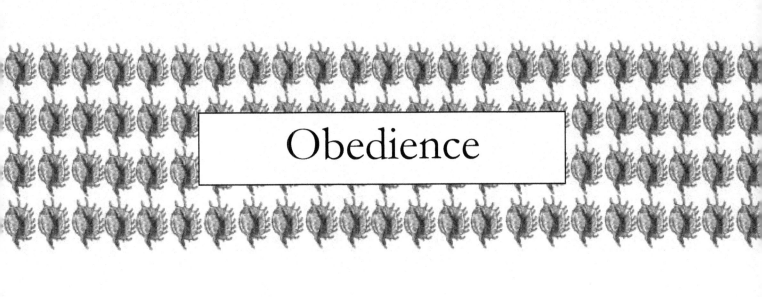

Obedience

There was once a father who had to go away on a business trip for a few months. Before he left he summoned his three sons, for he had instructions that he wanted them to follow while he was away.

To the eldest son he gave the instruction, "Redecorate my house."

To the middle son he gave the instruction, "Weed my garden."

To the youngest son he gave the instruction, "Do my laundry."

When the father returned home from his trip, he was eager to see how his sons had managed with the jobs that he had left them responsible for.

First, he checked his house. It was clean, the furniture had been arranged in a pleasing manner, and there were three beautiful new paintings on the wall. Next, he checked his garden. The lawn and flowerbeds had been paved over, and a wonderful brand new barbecue area installed. Finally, he checked his laundry. His white clothes were now a light pink, and some of his socks appeared to have shrunk.

The father summoned his sons and challenged them.

To the eldest son he said, "I asked you to redecorate the house, and when I return I find that you have just moved the furniture and put some paintings up. Explain yourself."

"Father," the eldest son said, "when you asked me to redecorate the house I realised that what you were really saying was that you felt that the house was looking a bit tired and needed some smartening up, so I gave everything a thorough clean, rearranged the furniture and bought some smart new paintings - with my own money, I might add."

To the middle son he said, "I asked you to weed my garden, and when I return I find that you have paved over my lawn and built a barbecue area. Explain yourself."

"Father," the middle son said, "when you asked me to weed the garden I realised that what you were really saying was that you wanted a tidy garden, so I arranged for the whole thing to be paved over. It was quite expensive and was a lot of work, but I think you'll agree it looks nice and tidy, and you certainly won't have any problems with weeds again. Plus, look at the barbecue area!"

To the youngest son he said, "I asked you to do my laundry, and when I return I find that my whites are pink and my socks have shrunk. Explain yourself."

"Father," the youngest son said, "I did the laundry, but once I forgot to separate the colours and, another time, I somehow managed to shrink your socks. I don't even know to this day how that happened. But, father, I did try."

Then the father looked at his sons and said, "I am going to change my will and leave everything to my youngest son, for I am well pleased with him."

The eldest and middle sons could not believe their ears, and they objected.

"What? You must be joking! He didn't even do the job properly, and even when he did he made a mess. You should have seen the state of the laundry room some days! Plus, look at your fantastic new barbecue area!"

And the father looked at the eldest and middle son and spoke:

"When I said 'redecorate my house' I meant 'redecorate my house', and when I said 'weed my garden' I meant 'weed my garden'. What you have said is true, but of the three of you, the youngest was the only one who actually did what I asked."

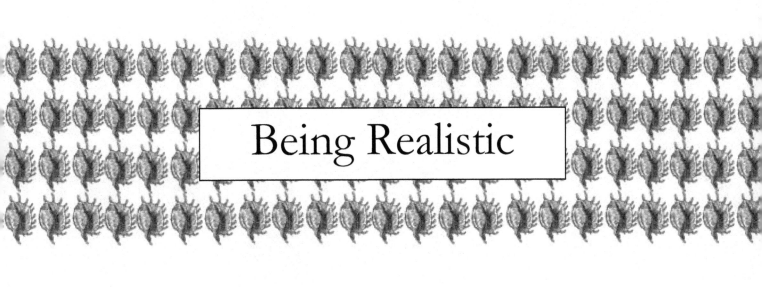

Being Realistic

So I said to Jesus, "What I'm saying is perfectly reasonable. It's not like I'm being difficult. It's just how things are in the world. I mean, I have to live here, don't I? There has to be a line somewhere, doesn't there? It's not as if I can do everything the way that you say. It's neither practical nor realistic. You have to be realistic. You do want followers, don't you? I know that you understand."

And Jesus said, "Sorry, I didn't catch any of that. Your chains were rattling too loudly."

Narrow Road

Mess and trouble, I had managed to get myself into a fix again. This time I had been caught with my hand in the cookie jar, which in itself wouldn't have been a huge crime if it wasn't for the fact that my sister keeps her collection of priceless diamonds in the cookie jar. It wasn't really my fault. If you want to keep your valuables safe, then surely you can do better than putting them in a cookie jar in a locked safe in a basement guarded by poisonous sharks. You call that security?

Once more I was hauled before the church elders and my wrist was slapped (this time they let me keep my sleeves rolled down).

"Thou shalt not steal! Young man, you need some guidance," they said.

"Who will help me?" I asked.

They wheeled out two respected church members. Once the two venerable gentlemen had removed their roller skates, they took their seats and looked at me.

"Choose one of these fine upstanding...no, beseated, members of our congregation to guide you."

"How can you help me?" I asked.

"I was once like you, son, a gentleman thief and rapscallion, but I am no longer this way. Well, mostly," said Jimmy the Lock.

"I have never been a thief," said Old Bill.

So, it was clear to me. Jimmy the Lock was my man. He knew what I had been through. He knew my shame. He had walked my path. He could guide me.

All went well for a while, until, mess and trouble, I found myself in another fix. I was receiving a medal for my exploits as a great war hero when it was publicly revealed that I had never actually been to war. When the recruiters had come round I had sent my pet goldfish to the door in my place. Little Bubbles was halfway through his third tour of duty. As for me, I had never fired a gun in anger, or in my garden or anywhere really. Perhaps I shouldn't have claimed to have single-handedly rescued four hundred soldiers from a burning motorcycle?

Once more I was hauled up before the church elders and had my knuckles rapped (it would have hurt more if I hadn't kept my gloves on).

"Thou shalt not bear false witness! Young man, you need some guidance," they said.

"Who will help me?" I asked.

They dusted off two respected church members. Once the two distinguished gentlemen had stopped sneezing, they took their seats and looked at me.

"Hey, put those seats down!" said the church elders.

"I was once like you, a liar and a cheat, but I am no longer this way. Well, mostly," said Trevor McFibber.

"I have never been a liar," said Old Bill.

So, Trevor McFibber was the one for me. He knew what I had been through. He knew my shame. He had walked my path. He could guide me.

But you know what's coming next, don't you? That's right, mess and trouble. I got myself into another sticky situation. All that I had done was make a generous donation to the local aged care charity. The problem was that my parents weren't too pleased, seeing as how they were the donation. The charity wasn't happy either, as they only fetched twenty-five pence on eBay. I told them that they should have let me write the listing.

Anyway, again I was dragged before the church elders to have my legs waxed (after all, summer is on the way).

"Thou shalt honour thy father and mother! Young man, you need a good whipping, but since we had to sell our whip to raise money to repair the church roof, you'll have to settle for some guidance," they said.

"Who will help me?" I asked.

They rolled out two respected church members. Once the two fine gentleman had stood up and brushed themselves down, they took their seats and looked at me.

"Choose one of them to help you, though we really don't see the point," the church elders muttered under their collective breath.

"I was once like you, a disrespectful cad and general scumbag, but I am no longer this way. Well, mostly," said Sebastian Sludge.

"I have never done anything quite so slimy as that," said Old Bill.

Sebastian Sludge has to be the one, doesn't he? He knew what I had been through. He knew my shame. He had walked my path. He could guide me.

No worries, mate. At least not for a short while. Until, mess and trouble, I was caught red-handed trying to shoplift a tin of maroon paint. To make matters worse, as the police escorted me from the premises, I bumped into Apostle Paul.

"Idiot!" Apostle Paul said, as he slapped me in the face. "You should have sought advice from the one who had made a habit of avoiding sin!"

"But...but...but he hadn't shared my failings," I objected.

He replied, "What's more important, being understood or being changed?"

The Expected Guest

The nameless servant removed the Baron's empty breakfast plate without a word, just as the Baron dismissed the nameless servant without a word.

"Are you going to the gates today?" said the Baroness from across the table.

"Of course," he said, standing up and signalling for his cloak of office.

"What time will you be back?" his wife said.

"Sunset, as yesterday, and the day before that, and the day before that. In fact, as every day for the last five weeks," the Baron muttered, exiting the dining room and heading for the hallway.

***

The sun had begun to sluggishly push its way through the crenellations on the city walls as the Baron and his party made their way down the hill towards the marketplace. Despite the early hour, the city was good and alive, as the citizens began the work of another day. The Baron moved through the streams of people on the streets, his entourage shoving and forcibly encouraging the citizens to step aside for their appointed leader. It didn't take long for the hill to level out and the narrow passage to open up into the marketplace, the heart of the city. Merchants were overseeing their stalls, screaming at the workers. Servants and craftsmen of all disciplines were already milling around, competing for that early morning bargain. Of course, the beggars were also already out in force. The smell alone was an education, the Baron thought to himself, shaking his head as he veered to the left and began the walk down the slight incline that would lead to the city gates. Even before he arrived, he could see the gathering. Musicians waiting with instruments at the ready, a small group of servants preparing food; two of the Archbishop's slaves standing patiently holding a rolled-up banner. The Baron performed a quick head count as he approached. The usual suspects, he thought. The Lady and her clerk, the Captain of the Militia and the Archbishop. But where was The Chief Tax Collector? He'd been there every day for the past five weeks. Surely not him too?

The assembled leaders turned to greet the Baron as he arrived.

"Where is Smithersby?" were the first words out of his mouth.

"Where do you think?" said the Lady. "He sends his apologies, of course, like the others." The Baron nodded. He'd stopped being disappointed weeks ago. It used to be different.

***

The messengers had started arriving at the city gates months ago. At first the message was simple, but clear.

"The King is coming."

This had sent the city into a panic. The King was coming here? They all knew that he made his way around the kingdom when he could, visiting his holdings and communing with the rulers of the populace, but it had been years since he had visited this city.

As the days went by, the messengers became more specific.

"He is coming soon."

"Get ready. Prepare the way. He will be here in a few weeks."

"He is nearly here. Keep watch and be alert."

After that last warning, no other messengers had come. But the city was already prepared. As the messages became more urgent, the leaders of the city became more organised. They resolved that, each day, they would wait at the city gates in order to greet their liege when he arrived. They would give him the welcome his majesty deserved, and he would see that the people of this city were loyal and worthy subjects.

The first day, the one after the arrival of the last messenger, they were all present. Everyone who was anyone in the city was at the gates, waiting for the King to arrive. The Baron, as the head of the city, took pride of place in the gathered throng, but they were all there. The various Guild leaders, the Chief Tax Collector, the assorted nobles who had made the city their home. All of them. They had made sure that there was food and music and gifts and banners to welcome the King when he arrived. But he didn't come that day.

The next day was the same. The crowd gathered, and prepared to greet their King, but he did not come that day. The watchers on the walls reported no sign of a royal procession. There were no more messengers either. Nothing.

The third day was the same as the one before it. The fourth day too.

By the fifth day, the crowd was noticeably smaller. Some of the Guild leaders had excused themselves. After all, they had jobs to do and the city depended on them. Of course they sent a few of their servants to help with the food and the music, but they themselves were conspicuous by their absence.

Day by day the crowd shrank as the leaders of the city resumed their daily business. They pledged that as soon as they heard word from the gate they would move with great haste to greet the King, but in the meantime they had things to do. The city depended on them, and surely the King would understand.

After five weeks of this the crowd at the gate could no longer be called a crowd. The Baron was there, of course, and so were the faithful ones with a small retinue of servants to provide food and entertainment, but that was all. From so many to so few in the space of five weeks.

***

"Any sign?" the Baron asked the others.

"Nothing," said the Archbishop.

"Perhaps he isn't coming. I mean, perhaps he will never come," the Lady said, putting into words the thoughts that they had all entertained.

"Patience and faithfulness, that is what our King requires," snapped the Archbishop.

"Indeed," said the Captain of the Militia, "I am sure we all heard about what happened...to the others."

They remembered in silence. The Captain was referring to a story that had reached their city the previous year. Apparently the King had arrived at one of the neighbouring cities and found his way barred. They weren't ready for his arrival, and they didn't welcome him. The Baron had heard a rumour that they'd even refused to let him enter. Either way, according to the story, the King and the soldiers that travelled with him had laid siege to the city and put its rulers to the sword. It was the type of story that nobles didn't like to reflect on.

The King had a reputation as a fearsome warrior. This reputation was beyond doubt, and well earned. The legends of his campaigns filled many an evening's conversation amongst the old warhorses at the taverns. He had more or less carved out his kingdom with his sword. Only a fool would dare to oppose him on the battlefield. There were no fools in this city.

"I'm sure they deserved it," said the Captain of the Militia after a moment's thought. "His wise judgements are as renowned as his military leadership."

They all nodded sagely. He had ruled well over the years and was well thought of amongst his subjects. Travellers from other cities often brought tales of his patient, gracious way of resolving issues and turning enemies into friends. He barely needed his army to keep the peace within his own borders. Barely.

However, it would not do to presume. That was why, even after five weeks, the Baron still maintained his vigil at the city gates. They would not be found wanting.

"I hear," said the Lady, suddenly, "that he even knows the deepest thoughts and desires of all his subjects."

There was silence at this pronouncement. The Baron took some pleasure from observing that even the Archbishop turned an interesting crimson colour.

"I have heard that rumour too," said the Archbishop eventually.

They all had. Surely it wasn't possible. Surely that was too much, even for the King. Surely it was only a rumour. But you couldn't be totally sure. Not with him. He really was remarkable.

"Well, he will find nothing to trouble him here," said the Baron, and he almost believed it.

***

The sun began to dip below the horizon.

"Another day wasted," said the Lady evenly, ignoring the glare that the Archbishop gave her. She turned sharply and began the long journey back to her villa on the other side of the city, snapping her fingers as she went. Her clerk, along with a motley collection of servants holding food and musical instruments, surged after her, like ducklings following their mother.

"I will see you tomorrow," said the Archbishop pointedly. The Baron nodded, as did the Captain of the Militia.

The two slaves clutching the banner followed their master as he plodded into the crowded street leading to the market. Pausing only to swipe at a passing beggar child with his staff, he waddled off in the direction of the cathedral.

The Baron and the Captain dismissed the remaining servants, and bid each other good night.

"Perhaps," said the Captain, his eyes locked with the Baron's, "it would not be so bad if he never arrived."

The Baron said nothing, but he knew exactly what the Captain meant. If all the stories were true and all the legends had foundation then maybe it would be better for them if the far-away King never became the nearby King. True, they were not so bad, as cities go. They paid their taxes on time. They didn't make trouble. They were loyal and given to genuine royalist sentiment, but still, who knew what he'd make of it all. The problem was that the King was unpredictable. Not arbitrary, but unpredictable. For a moment the Baron considered pouring out all of these concerns to the Captain, but the moment passed.

"Tomorrow then," he said instead.

"Aye," said the Captain, smiling and saluting. "Tomorrow."

As the Captain headed off to the barracks, the Baron signalled one of the guards at the city gate and addressed him, assuming his attention.

"As usual, if the night watchmen see or hear anything at all I am to be woken at once. At once, you understand?"

"Yes, my lord," said the guard, bowing low.

The Baron nodded his approval, and turned for home.

***

He entered his mansion and, as usual, was greeted by a serving girl carrying a large bowl of fresh water. He washed his hands, face and feet, and removed his cloak.

"Dinner is ready?"

"Yes, my lord," said the serving girl, averting her gaze.

The Baron entered the dining room to see his wife, as usual, sitting in her place.

"I assume it was another fruitless day," she said, as her husband took his seat opposite her. He ignored his wife's comment and instead summoned a servant.

"I am hungry. Bring our food now."

"I don't know why you bother," his wife said, as the servant came forward and placed a large bowl of hot broth in front of each of them.

"Because the day I don't bother is the day that the King arrives. I guarantee it. And if we do not welcome him then I dread to think what will happen," said the Baron, lifting a full spoon of the nourishing soup into his mouth. He swallowed, and almost instantly felt better as the tasty food began to soothe his weary body.

"Surely his majesty will understand. You have a city to run," his wife said.

"That serving girl at the door," said the Baron, changing the subject. "Is she new? I didn't recognise her."

"Yes. There were some new slaves at the market today."

"Honestly, my dear, I can't keep up. It seems like we have new servants every few days."

"Well, you know how it is. It's so hard to get good help these days," his wife said, smiling at him. The Baron smiled back as he scooped up the napkin by his bowl to wipe his lips and, as he did so, something small fell from the cloth and tinkled onto the floor.

He bent down, gripped the item between his fingers and lifted it to his eye.

"What's that?" said his wife, craning to see.

It was a ring, a golden band with a single small amethyst set in it. The Baron peered intently at the stone.

"What is it?" his wife repeated, standing up now, trying to get a better look.

"A ring," her husband said, engrossed by the tiny object in his hand.

There was something else. Something etched into the gemstone, small as it was. A symbol, one that the Baron instantly recognised. The royal seal. A chill ran down his spine.

"That servant." He looked up at his wife. "The one who's been serving me at the table recently. Where did you get him?"

"Me?" His wife looked troubled. "It wasn't me. I thought that you'd bought him."

"How long has he been here?" the Baron said, his voice barely a whisper.

"I don't know." His wife slumped back into her chair and bit her lip. "Two weeks or so."

Two weeks!

The Baron sat, terrified, as he tried desperately to recall the subject of conversations at the meal table over the past fourteen days - every ill-chosen comment, every harsh and unfair word to a servant. Then he stood up and turned towards the kitchen. His first few steps were quick, but by the time that he reached the door he was running.

"Your majesty!" he called out as he sprinted down the steps, along the corridor and round the corner. "Your majesty!"

He crashed through the door into the kitchen, and was greeted by a handful of astonished looking servants.

"Your majesty!" he called again, hoping against hope, but all he saw were the familiar faces of his kitchen staff.

"Where is he? Where is he?" the Baron said, grabbing one of the cooks by the shoulders. The cook shook his head and pointed at the door in the wall, the one that led to the courtyard outside.

It was open, swinging gently back and forth in the breeze. The Baron rushed to the doorway and peered into the outer darkness, but he knew that it was too late. The nameless servant had vanished into the night.

CONCLUSION

What now?

"Those who have ears, let them hear," said Jesus.

And what have you heard?

"Come all you who are thirsty,

come to the waters;

and you who have no money,

come, buy and eat!

Come, buy wine and milk without money and without cost.

Why spend money on what is not bread,

and your labour on what does not satisfy?

Listen, listen to me, and eat what is good,

and your soul will delight in the richest of fare.

Give ear and come to me;

hear me, that your soul may live

I will make an everlasting covenant with you,

my faithful love promised to David."

Isaiah 55:1-3

ABOUT THE AUTHOR

James has had a variety of interesting learning experiences in his life, some from being a Baptist minister in the UK and then some from being a member of Cornerstone Community, a mission and discipleship community in Australia. He fancies himself as something of a storyteller, and this book is his second attempt to put some of the things he's learnt into words. James currently lives in Canterbury with his wife and five (yes, five) children.

For more information about either of The Listening Books, or to sign up to James's blog, visit
www.thelisteningbook.org.uk

"Does not wisdom call?
Does not understanding raise her voice?"

Lightning Source UK Ltd.
Milton Keynes UK
UKOW04f0516020217

293428UK00007B/122/P